W9-CLE-833

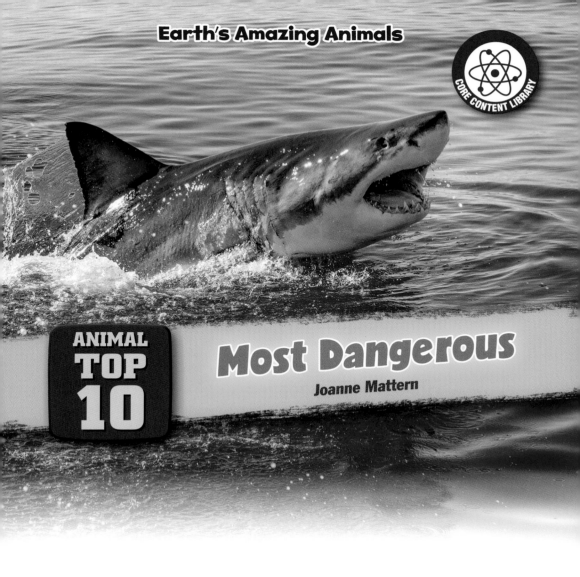

CORE CONTENT LIBRARY

ANIMAL
TOP
10

Most Dangerous

Joanne Mattern

RED
CHAIR
•PRESS•

Earth's Amazing Animals is produced and published by Red Chair Press:

Red Chair Press LLC   PO Box 333   South Egremont, MA 01258-0333

www.redchairpress.com

Publisher's Cataloging-in-Publication Data
Names: Mattern, Joanne, 1963–
Title: Animal top 10. Most dangerous / Joanne Mattern.
Other Titles: Animal top ten. Most dangerous | Most dangerous | Core content library.

Description: South Egremont, MA : Red Chair Press, [2019] | Series: Earth's amazing animals | Includes glossary, Power Word science term etymology, fact and trivia sidebars. | Interest age level: 007-010. | Includes bibliographical references and index. | Summary: "Which animal is called Black Death? Did you know one of the most dangerous animals eats only grass and plants? Some animals kill by biting and fighting, others are deadly to touch!"--Provided by publisher.

Identifiers: LCCN 2018955614 | ISBN 9781634406901 (library hardcover) | ISBN 9781634407861 (paperback) | ISBN 9781634406963 (ebook)

Subjects: LCSH: Animal defenses--Juvenile literature. | Animals--Juvenile literature. | CYAC: Animal defenses. | Animals.

Classification: LCC QL751.5 .M383 2019 (print) | LCC QL751.5 (ebook) | DDC 591.47--dc23

Illustrations by Tim Haggerty.

Photo credits: cover, pp. 1, 3, 5 (top, bottom), 6–9, 12–15, 17, 19–22, 30, 33, 34, 36–39 iStock; pp. 5 (center), 29, 31 Shutterstock; p. 10 © National Geographic Image Collection/Alamy; p. 11 © Joao Burini/Minden Pictures; p. 16 © Joe Belanger/Alamy; p. 17 © Robert F. Sisson/Getty Images; p. 18 © Fred Bavendam/Minden Pictures; p. 23 © Jurgen Freund/Minden Pictures; p. 24 © Nature Picture Library/Alamy; pp. 25–27 © Kim Taylor/Minden Pictures; p. 35 © Martin Dohrn/Minden Pictures.

Printed in United States of America

0519 1P CGF19

Table of Contents

Introduction

The animal world can be a very scary place. Our planet is full of predators with long claws, sharp teeth, powerful bodies, and **venomous** bites. Most of these animals are dangerous because they are looking for **prey**. Others are just trying to survive by fighting back against another animal or even against a person. And some animals are dangerous and deadly for more surprising reasons.

Dangerous animals come in all shapes and sizes. Some live in the ocean, while others live on land. Others fly through the air. Wherever you look, there is bound to be something dangerous lurking there.

We've put together a list of the Top Ten Most Dangerous Animals. Some of our choices might surprise you! Let's take a look at the scariest and most dangerous creatures on Planet Earth!

And the Winners Are...

Here are our choices for the Top 10 Most Dangerous Animals. Turn the pages to find out more about each of these creepy creatures.

10. The Great White Shark

9. The Cape Buffalo

8. The Brazilian Wandering Spider

7. The Hippopotamus

6. The Cone Snail

5. The Saltwater Crocodile

4. The Box Jellyfish

3. The Tsetse Fly

2. The Black Mamba

1. The Mosquito

#9

#8

#2

10 The Great White Shark

The great white shark has a bad reputation. This fish is certainly dangerous. Its giant mouth is filled with more than 300 teeth. Each tooth can be more than three inches (7.5 cm) long. This powerful predator has killed more than 300 people since the late 1500s and attacked many more.

Great white sharks live in oceans all over the world. They usually live in colder waters near the coast. These fish can be up to 18 feet (5.5 m) long. Instead of humans, great whites usually eat seals, sea lions, and small whales.

Fear Fact

A great white has a great sense of smell. A shark can detect one drop of blood in 25 gallons of water.

9 The Cape Buffalo

This animal's nickname is The Black Death, so you know it is dangerous! The Cape buffalo is big and powerful. These creatures can weigh more than 1,700 pounds (770 kg) and stand up to six feet (2 m) tall. And then there are those horns. A Cape buffalo's horns can grow up to five feet (1.5 m) long.

Cape buffalo are one of the most dangerous animals in Africa. They will not hesitate to **charge** other animals, even lions. Every year they kill more humans in Africa than any other animal.

Fear Fact

Cape buffalo are dangerous, but they are not predators. These animals are herbivores and only eat grass.

8 The Brazilian Wandering Spider

There are many venomous spiders in the world, but few are as dangerous as the Brazilian wandering spider.

This spider was first discovered in Brazil, but it also lives in other parts of South and Central America. They are also called "banana spiders" because they often hide in bunches of bananas.

This spider grows up to five inches (13 cm) long and has long, hairy legs. Like most spiders, it has six small eyes and two big eyes. The Brazilian wandering spider does not wait for prey in its web. Instead, it walks around the floor of the rainforest, hunting for its prey. This spider's favorite foods are crickets and other large insects. It also eats small lizards and mice.

A person who is bitten by one of these spiders is in big trouble. The venom makes a bite extremely painful and can damage the brain. If the victim does not get **antivenin** in time, he or she can die.

7 The Hippopotamus

The hippopotamus is big and heavy, but is it really dangerous? The answer is yes. Hippos are responsible for more deaths in Africa than any other animal. About 3,000 people are killed by hippos every year.

Hippos are dangerous because they are very **aggressive.** They often fight with each other and with other animals. If people bother a group of hippos, the animals will charge them. And since a hippo can run as fast as 14 miles (22 km) an hour, it is almost impossible for a person to get away. Hippos will even attack boats full of people sailing down rivers!

Power Word: From two ancient Greek words, *hippo* for horse and *potamus* for river, the hippopotamus is often called a river horse.

A hippopotamus weighs about 3,000 pounds
(1,360 kg). These animals live in large groups.
They spend a lot of their
time lying in the mud or
in the water. This helps
them keep cool. At
night, they come on
land and eat grass
and other plants.

6 The Cone Snail

Is the most venomous animal of Earth a snake? Is it a spider? Nope! It's a snail. The cone snail lives in warm ocean waters. It kills its prey with a nasty combination of teeth and venom.

A cone snail crawls across a reef looking for prey to paralyze and eat.

This cone snail has caught a fish to eat.

Cone snails hide on rocks or coral reefs or bury themselves in sand to wait for their prey. When a fish swims past, the cone snail bites it with teeth that are like tiny needles. These teeth inject a powerful venom that **paralyzes** the prey right away. Then the cone snail can take its time eating its dinner. It's important that the venom act right away. Otherwise the fish could quickly swim away from the slow-moving snail.

Pretty to look at, deadly to touch!

Cone snails aren't just dangerous to fish. They can kill people too. Divers can be stung if they pick up the cone snail's colorful shell. There is no antivenin against the cone snail's poison. Although cone snails haven't killed a lot of people, about 65 percent of those who are bitten die.

Fear Fact

A cone snail is always growing new teeth.

5 The Saltwater Crocodile

Most crocodiles are dangerous, but none are as deadly as the saltwater crocodile. These giants are the largest members of the crocodile family. They measure more than 17 feet (5 m) long and weigh 1,000 to 2,000 pounds (450–900 kg). They live in northern Australia and parts of India and Southeast Asia.

The saltwater crocodile is the largest of all reptiles.

Saltwater crocodiles are **carnivores.** They **ambush** their prey, lying in wait under the water or near the shore. When its prey gets too close, the crocodile grabs it and drags it under the water in a flash. Their prey includes large animals like wild boars, water buffaloes, and even sharks.

Anything near the water can be dinner.

Another deadly fact about this crocodile is its jaws are extremely strong. Once they bite down, it is very hard to open their jaws. A crocodile's mouth is also filled with lots of sharp teeth. This predator can tear its prey apart. Even humans aren't safe from this scary croc. Saltwater crocodiles kill many people every year.

The Box Jellyfish

The box jellyfish looks a little weird and maybe even cute. But don't let its looks fool you. This jellyfish is one of the deadliest animals in the world.

Box jellyfish have long tentacles. One jellyfish can have up to 15 tentacles, and tentacles can be ten feet (3 m) long. Each tentacle is covered with thousands of tiny darts filled with poison.

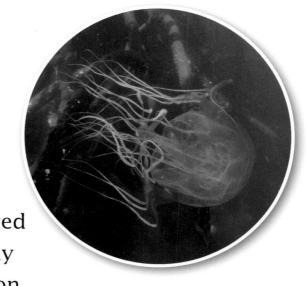

When the jellyfish's tentacle touches someone, the poison is injected into the person's blood. Instantly, the poison causes the person's blood pressure to get extremely high. Soon afterward, the victim's heart may stop. All this can take just two minutes. Even if a victim is lucky enough to survive, he or she will be in terrible pain for weeks. About 20 to 40 people die from box jellyfish stings every year. Most stings happen in the waters around Australia and the Philippines.

Unlike most other jellyfish, which just float in the water, box jellyfish are good swimmers. As they swim, they hunt their prey, which includes shrimp and small fish.

Fear Fact

Box jellyfish have 24 eyes.

A box jellyfish with its prey

3 The Tsetse Fly

So far almost all the animals we've talked about have been BIG and bad. But one of the deadliest animals on the planet is actually quite small. The little insect called the tsetse has had a deadly effect on humans.

Unlike other insects, tsetse flies give birth to live young. The babies start as eggs but stay inside the mother's body until they reach the larval stage.

A Tsetse Fly larva hatching

Tsetse flies live in Africa. These flies like to bite humans and animals and suck their blood. A tsetse fly's bite is painful, because the insect has sharp teeth that cut into the victim's skin like tiny saws.

Sucking blood is bad enough, but a tsetse fly's bite also spreads disease. One of the most dangerous diseases spread by tsetse flies is called sleeping sickness. The disease starts with a fever, headache, and body aches. Soon the victim is tired all the time. If the disease reaches the brain, the victim will die.

A hundred years ago, hundreds of thousands of people died from sleeping sickness each year. Methods of controlling flies and better medicine have dropped the death toll. Still, more than 3,000 people die of sleeping sickness each year!

2 The Black Mamba

Many snakes are dangerous and scary. But the black mamba beats them all. This snake is big, fast, and aggressive. And its venom is almost 100 percent deadly.

Black mambas live in Africa. They are the largest African snake and can measure up to 14 feet (4 m) long, although most are about 8 feet (2.5 m) long. These snakes aren't black. Instead, they are usually brown, gray, or olive green. They get their name from the blue-black color inside their mouth. If an animal or a person is unlucky enough to see that black color, he or she is in big trouble.

The "black" of the Black Mamba only shows when they open their mouth.

A black mamba's venom affects the nervous system and the heart. Without antivenin, a black mamba's bite can kill a person in about 20 minutes.

Unfortunately, more people are moving into places where black mambas live. This makes it more likely that people will be bitten by this very dangerous snake.

Black mambas are carnivores. They usually eat small mammals and birds. The snake hunts by injecting its prey with venom and then letting it go. Then the snake follows its victim until it dies. Then the black mamba eats its meal whole. This snake can unhinge its jaw to fit an animal more than four times the size of its head into its mouth. Some reports say black mambas have been found with whole parrots in their stomachs.

A Black Mamba eating a bat

1 The Mosquito

And now, we present the #1 most dangerous animal—the MOSQUITO!

Yes, the mosquito. The annoying pest that can ruin a summer night outside kills a *million* people every year. Mosquitoes have killed more people than all the wars in history combined. That high death toll comes from the fact that the mosquito spreads many different and deadly diseases.

There are about 3,500 species of mosquito, but not all feast on human blood. Only females of some species bite humans. Females need the protein found in blood to help their eggs develop.

Humans make a tasty target!

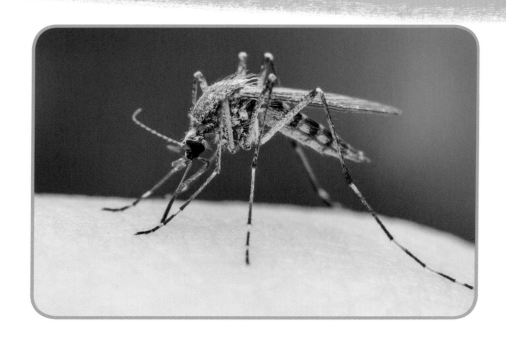

A female mosquito's mouth has a long sucking tube. She punctures the skin with the sharp point on the end of the tube and sucks out the blood.

The problem is that while the mosquito is biting a human or animal, it is also spreading germs. These germs can cause many different diseases, including malaria and yellow fever. These diseases have killed *millions of people* throughout history. More recently, mosquitoes have spread new diseases such as the Zika and West Nile viruses.

Mosquitos have a short lifespan. Males only live about two weeks. Females live for about a month. It only takes four to 14 days for a mosquito to complete its life cycle from egg to adult. A female mosquito can start biting people just two days after she becomes an adult. From then on, she is an agent of death and danger.

Fear Fact

Some scientists think we should get rid of all mosquitoes. However, these insects do provide food for many animals including opossums, spiders, salamanders, frogs, and fish.

Mosquito emerging from pupa at water surface

Dangerous Animal Runners-Up

Here are a few more creatures that didn't quite make the Top 10, but are still pretty scary!

African lion

Komodo dragon

Poison dart frog

Pufferfish

What's Your Top 10?

You've seen our list of the Top 10 Most Dangerous Animals and some runners-up as well. Now it's your turn! Which animals in this book do YOU think are the most dangerous? Are there other animals that you think should be on the list? Check your library or go on the Internet and find photos and information on all that's dangerous in the animal world. Then make your own Top 10 list!

Glossary

aggressive likely to attack

ambush to make a surprise attack

antivenin medicine that stops the action of venom

carnivores animals that only eat meat

charge to rush forward in an attack

detect to find

herbivores animals that only eat plants

larval in insects, the stage that comes after the egg

paralyzes makes it impossible to move part of the body

predators animals that eat other animals for food

prey animals eaten by other animals for food

venomous able to inject venom

Learn More in the Library

Are there other animals that you think should be on the list? Discover more about our most dangerous animals, then search for more animals to add to your list!

DK Books. *Sharks and Other Deadly Ocean Creatures.* DK Publishing, 2016.

Franchino, Vicky. *Black Mambas (Nature's Children).* Scholastic, 2015.

Stewart, Melissa. *Deadliest Animals.* Algonquin Young Readers, 2017.

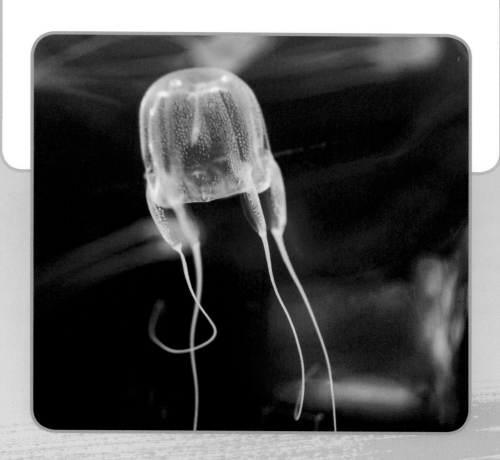

Index

About the Author

Joanne Mattern is the author of nearly 350 books for children and teens. She began writing when she was a little girl and just never stopped! Joanne loves nonfiction because she enjoys bringing science topics to life and showing young readers that nonfiction is full of compelling stories! Joanne lives in the Hudson Valley of New York State with her husband, four children, and several pets!